Come Through
Life's Sucker Punches
BRILLIANT, not BROKEN.

Brilliantly Resilient

Reset, Rise and Reveal Your Brilliance

Mary Fran Bontempo
& Kristin Smedley

Brilliantly Resilient Publications

For everyone who has been hit by a sucker punch or found themselves in the middle of a train wreck.

You are

BRILLIANTLYRESILIENT!

Praise for
Brilliantly Resilient

"Resilience is essential to success. But when you take it a step further and add your Brilliance—that's bringing the heat! With heart and humor, Kristin and Mary Fran have taken their sucker punches and created a Brilliantly Resilient mission that proves everyone can Reset, Rise and Reveal their Brilliance to the world. A must read!"

John Lee Dumas
Host of Entrepreneurs on Fire
https://www.eofire.com/

"As someone who is alive today because I turned my hope for a cure for my disease into action, I didn't think I could be more driven to take action. Somehow Kristin Smedley and Mary Fran Bontempo managed to motivate and inspire me through Brilliantly Resilient to fight harder than ever, and they provide the tools and strategies we all need to uncover our Resilience and begin to share our Brilliance with the world."

David Fajgenbaum, MD, MBA, MSc
National Bestselling Author
Chasing My Cure: A Doctor's Race to Turn Hope Into Action www.ChasingMyCure.com

"Resetting your mindset is no easy task. But with Brilliantly Resilient, Mary Fran and Kristin help lead you to uncover your Brilliance by taking small, accessible and actionable steps leading to big results that reflect your values, beliefs and strengths. They're also funny, approachable and completely relatable. 'Game Changers' for sure!"

Rob Angel
Author of Game Changer and Creator of Pictionary
https://robangel.com/

"I am thrilled that Mary Fran and Kristin are writing again all with the intention to propel women into believing in themselves, honoring their journey and bravely moving forward towards their goals. Their movement is inspiring, and they are filled with such deep passion for making a positive difference that it moves and makes those around them lift up and inspire others to do the same."

Violette de Ayala
Founder of FemCity,
Best Selling Author, The Self-Guided Guru
https://www.violettedeayala.com/

"Resilience has never been more critical to our existence. In this time of daily...even hourly change...the ability to adapt and embrace the growth opportunities is the difference between those who survive and those who thrive. Mary Fran and Kristin know from unique experience how to flex those resilience muscles. Even better, they have the special ability to translate those experiences into tactical development for the rest of us!"

Tiffany O'Donnell
CEO, Women Lead Change
www.wlcglobal.org

"You know those women you're just dying to spend a night over a pitcher of margaritas? That would be Mary Fran and Kristin. This dynamic duo is truly a match made in heaven. Fortunately for us, they're doing their divine work right here on earth. They share their brilliance to lift us up and brighten our spirits at just the right time. Their powerful stories will make you laugh, and they'll make you cry. They will open your eyes to what is possible when you're a Fierce Midlife Woman who believes in the power of Resilience. We are born brilliant. We simply forget as we get older. I believe the lower we fall, the higher we bounce. Mary Fran and Kristin are proving that to be true beyond measure. Their stories are wildly different, each one a combination of heartbreak & inspiration. They share a common thread in two women pushed to the edge who, ultimately, learned how to fly. They are living examples of the power of the indomitable human spirit. Buy the book and rediscover how Brilliantly Resilient you are!"

Catherine Grace O'Connell
Founder & CEO
Catherine Grace O and Mastering Modern Midlife
https://catherinegraceo.com/

"Kristin Smedley and Mary Fran Bontempo are Brilliantly Resilient and relentless in their pursuit to make the world a better place by sharing their process for overcoming life's sucker punches and train wrecks. They provide key strategies to help one Go Get It in life despite challenges. A great book by some great ladies! Go get it!"

Chip Baker
Educator, Author, Creator of
Chip Baker – The Success Chronicles
https://www.facebook.com/chipbakertsc/

"You hear about women with the strength, confidence, and pizzazz that Mary Fran and Kristin embody, and you whisper to yourself, 'They are beyond me,' or 'I can't be like that.' Then, you interact with their honesty, humor, imperfection, and joy, and you say, 'They get it.' This is a revelation everyone should give herself a chance to have. I found myself digging deeper into my own story than ever before, all because of what Mary Fran and Kristin coaxed me to consider. I found myself connecting dots and releasing shadowed disappointments. Oh, yes, the journey these two lay out is one worth taking!"

Kathy Nimmer—Award-winning teacher,
Author & Motivational Speaker
https://www.amazon.com/Minutes-Eternity-Light-Kathy-Nimmer/dp/1598582542

"If life has thrown you a curveball, there is comfort in knowing that other people get benched too. What Mary Fran and Kristin have put together in 'Brilliantly Resilient' is light in a dark place--filled with stories of how to find your spark then how to light that sucker up! You will find compassion, courage, and the Brilliance of how to become more Resilient. Your life is not defined by your challenges; it's defined by the choices you make to be Brilliantly Resilient."

Nicole Simonin
Health and Fitness Coach & Author of
The No Fuss, No Mess, Shape it Up Cookbook
www.ShapeItUpFitness.com

"When you are going through a difficult time, Mary Fran Bontempo and Kristin Smedley are the women to get you through. They've either 'been there done that' or been close enough to say, 'let's figure out a way to get you through this.' Now, they've put all their experience and chutzpa in a book. They will remind you of what you've survived in the past, your power and your gifts - and then inspire you to reach beyond your current struggle to step into your divine brilliance. When you need strength, they lend you theirs. These women swam in waters they never intended and came out gold medalists and they want nothing more than for you to do the same. When life gives you a whole pile of 'what the hell am I going to do with all of this?' this book will give you a little nudge (or a knock on the head) to help you say 'I've got this.'"

Jennifer Gardella Social Media Expert
https://jennifergardella.com/

"Kristin and Mary Fran are a perfect combo of humor, realness, and go-get-em'-ness. Through the Brilliantly Resilient process, they motivate and challenge us to uncover our Resilience, take action and embrace our own special Brilliance to share our gifts with the world. These are two courageous women. I'm proud to be a member of the Brilliantly Resilient tribe!"

Ming Shelby
Speaker, Teacher, Founder of
Courage Up Podcast
https://www.mingshelby.com/

Table of Contents

Introduction

Have you ever seen people together—either as a couple or friends—and wondered, *How the heck did they end up with each other?* We get that a lot. Friends, family, pretty much everyone who knows us has the same reaction when they learn we're not only friends, but we've created Brilliantly Resilient together. Huh? You two? You work together? Sometimes even we don't understand why it works. But it does.

It's hard to imagine two more wildly different people than us—Kristin Smedley and Mary Fran Bontempo. We're polar opposites. We attended the wedding of a mutual friend once, and the picture from that night says it all: Kristin is in a short, bright blue cocktail dress, long black hair flying, with sky—high heels. Mary Fran is wearing a floor-length, black gown, short blond hair carefully coiffed, with flat sandals peeking out from her dress. Kristin, by her own admission, is a delirious optimist; Mary Fran is far more cautious and, by her own admission, suspicious. (It's a by-product of her son's addiction. Don't judge.)

In the picture, we're not just smiling, we're laughing. We do that a lot, despite histories of train wrecks and sucker punches that brought each of us to our knees more than once.

That's where we found common ground. Our challenges were different—Kristin's two boys were born blind; and Mary Fran's son battled heroin addiction and alcoholism for years. In sharing our messes, we discovered that we had way more in common than our differences would indicate.

We're both fighters who had to pick ourselves up off the floor again and again, which we did for our kids. We might not have done it for ourselves alone, but our kids? Get out of the way—mama bears coming through. We share common values like kindness, truth, and faith, among others. And the faith part—oh goodness. We've both kicked, screamed, and shaken our fists at God, all while alternately begging for and demanding help, which we got, even if it wasn't the kind of help we wanted.

We share a teaching background, but perhaps more importantly, we share a desire or maybe even a need to help others, because neither of us wants anyone to feel the way we felt when slammed by a crisis. We learned that our crises didn't need to define us, nor become our entire stories. There was more, way more, after the sucker punches and train wrecks, and that's where Brilliantly Resilient was born.

Gaining that "more", after a sucker punch or train wreck doesn't happen by magic. It requires work. It's hard. But it is possible—and necessary if you don't want to turn into one of those people who whines their entire life about what happened to them and uses it as an excuse for never getting where they say they want to go.

We whine; make no mistake. But we give ourselves an allotted time to complain and then we smack ourselves (literally if necessary). We say, "Okay, snap out of it," and then we figure out what we can do to start to not only clean up the caca, but to climb out of the pit.

We both decided long ago that we don't like the pit. It's dark down there, and we both have shiny object syndrome. (Especially Mary Fran, who has a giant corkboard loaded with sparkly necklaces in her room.) We crave light and life, and we know it exists on the other side of a train wreck or sucker punch because we experienced those beatdowns and have not only lived but thrived to tell the story.

That's what's different about being Brilliantly Resilient. Being Resilient is one thing, but being Brilliant after a gut punch? Now that's cool.

There's one other thing we have in common. We both agree that we're not special. That is, we've decided that we're pretty fantastic, but so is everyone else; they just haven't figured out exactly how. We're still learning, too. Every day, we learn something new about how to be Resilient and how to uncover our Brilliance. And we're having a blast.

Believe us, if we can be Brilliantly Resilient, so can you. There's a process to it, and the good news is that it can be learned and practiced. And yes, you'll need practice—we still do. Join us. We love adding to our tribe. We love to laugh, which we do a ton of, and we love to learn and pass on what we know, so everyone can be Brilliantly Resilient.

Don't waste another minute. Get reading, take notes, watch our show, listen to the podcast, join our Facebook Group. We're Kristin and Mary Fran. We're Brilliantly Resilient—and so are you.

CHAPTER 1

You Deserve Better

You know the feeling.

Things are going along fine. Life, if not fantastic, is pretty okay, and your biggest decision may be what to order for lunch. And then…it hits.

Seemingly out of nowhere, you're knocked off your feet by a sucker punch that not only takes the wind out of you, but takes away everything you thought you knew about yourself, your life, where you'd been, where you were going, and what you knew to be true. Or at least thought you knew.

Suddenly, you're navigating your own personal train wreck, with no idea of how to crawl through the twisted mess, let alone make everything all right— not that you're even sure what that means anymore. You don't know where to turn, and you can't possibly imagine how life will ever be good again.

But if you can be certain of only one thing, know this: You are not alone.

We are Mary Fran Bontempo and Kristin Smedley,

founders of Brilliantly Resilient, TEDx speakers, award-winning authors, Brilliantly Resilient LIVE online show and podcast hosts, as well as content, program, and workshop creators. Kristin founded a global rare eye disease patient organization, and Mary Fran is a sought-after advocate for families coping with substance abuse. We know our Brilliance, but we didn't always. In fact, both of us know what it feels like to be lost, afraid, unproductive, unsuccessful, and unhappy. That's a lot of yuck, but without it, there would have been no need for Resilience, the key to uncovering your Brilliance.

How can we talk about Brilliance when experiencing a metaphorical train wreck? Because we know that not only is discovering your Brilliance possible, the best place to start can be after the sucker punch lands—when you may be down, you may be questioning everything you ever thought you knew, but you are by no means out of the fight. In fact, your best rounds may be yet to come, with a championship belt just waiting for you to claim as your own.

Nothing we've done, from taking the TEDx stage to becoming in-demand speakers, influencers and advocates was ever part of the plans we had for our lives. And we mean NONE of it. What we've managed to create by uncovering our Resilience and discovering our Brilliance has all been a delightful surprise of sorts, because while the good stuff is really good, the bad stuff—our personal sucker punches and train wrecks—was really, really bad.

In working together and getting to know each other, we realized that although the details of our stories were different, we both kept coming back to the same underlying themes of Resetting with Resilience after our challenges, Rising to create something new, and finally, Revealing our Brilliance and sharing it with the world. Reset, Rise, Reveal. The Brilliantly Resilient roadmap.

Brilliantly Resilient. Yep, it has a nice ring to it, but it's more than that. Being Brilliantly Resilient means that not only are you capable of managing your challenges, but you can also use those same crises to uncover your power, your creativity, and your true identity, to build a life you never knew was possible.

And to those of you not experiencing a sucker punch or train wreck right now, YAHOO!!! We're thrilled for you! Congratulations! But we're willing to bet that even you can benefit from a little Brilliance in your life. Who can't?

Even when we're chugging along, relatively content, the opportunity to be Brilliant is always there, right behind the everyday, with sparkles, rainbows, and unicorns waiting to fly out and take you beyond the clouds…. Okay, no unicorns. But each and every one of us is capable of our own unique Brilliance, and honestly, it's your RESPONSIBILITY to share the very best you have to offer with the rest of us. We need you.

When the world experiences cosmic train wrecks along the lines of global pandemics and racial divisiveness, one of the buzz words that comes back into play is Resilience. These days, everyone is talking Resilience. What it is, how to find it, what to do with it.

According to Psychology Today, "Resilience is about getting through pain and disappointment without letting them crush your spirit." Pain, disappointment, and crush. Ugh. Yucky words. Yet, they are just as much a part of life as the good stuff. We could argue that pain and disappointment make the sweet stuff even sweeter. When we take an active part in refusing to be crushed by the ugly stuff, calling upon Resilience to get us up and back in the fight, we stake our claim to the good stuff. We deserve it, and by choosing Resilience, we let the universe know that we may go down, but we're sure as heck getting back up.

Our Brilliantly Resilient friend, mentor, and founder of EOFire, John Lee Dumas reminds us:

It's critical to understand the importance of Resilience. Getting sucker punched, failing, flopping, is part of everyone's journey. But for those who succeed, it's about getting up again, swinging that bat and eventually hitting that single, double, home run or maybe a grand slam on that next swing.

John Lee Dumas—EOFire

Resilience is how being Brilliantly Resilient begins. But it's not where it ends. If we stop at Resilience, we're stopping too soon. As JLD notes, it's about getting back up to try again. Because life is about more than just falling down and getting back up. Unless we go beyond simply getting up, we risk becoming a living punching bag, standing in place while waiting for the next blow to fall.

That's where Brilliance comes in. When we add

Brilliance to the equation, we open ourselves to the possibility of being made for more, and that we deserve better. More and better. Ming Shelby, of the Courage Up podcast, says:

I can do better; I deserve better.

Ming Shelby—Courage Up Podcast

We all deserve better. But better doesn't just fall in our laps. Heck, even if we're looking for it, it's not always easy to define what better is, let alone find it. So, we need to figure out how to hunt it down, to explore what it means to us, for us, in each of our lives, because our better may not be your better.

As we were working our way through our respective sucker punches and train wrecks, neither of us knew or even imagined, what our *better* world would look like. Actually, all we truly wanted was not horrible. But both of us experienced that tipping point, that place where everything just sucked so badly that we got mad as hell and decided we weren't going to take it anymore. (Well, mad and scared, both of which are wildly powerful motivators for action.)

We were at rock bottom, and with nothing to lose, we just decided to try anything and everything because, well, why the hell not?

We careened around for a long time, trying things, having successes, having failures (definitely more failures), and trying to figure out how to make something decent out of some terribly crappy circumstances.

Did we say it took a long time? It took a REALLY long time. As Kristin likes to say, we weren't always quick on the uptake. Slow learners, not the brightest bulbs—you get the idea. But now that we've compared notes and realized how we were both working the same type of system without even knowing each other, well NOW, we get it.

Uncovering your Resilience and discovering your Brilliance is a process, one we want to share with you throughout this Brilliantly Resilient series. There are steps, strategies, and tactics you can employ to uncover your Resilience and Brilliance and share your awesomeness with the world. We aren't gonna lie; it takes some effort. But it's SO worth it. And if WE can do it, YOU can do it too!

CHAPTER 2

You Are Resilient!

To begin, you need to understand this basic truth: You
have inherent Resilience. You were born with it. Everyone
is born with it. Think about it—you learned to walk and
speak. You didn't succeed at those things the first time
you tried them. You tried and failed repeatedly until you
figured it out and mastered it, without letting the failures
leading up to your success crush you and keep you from
trying again.

As children, we understand without even thinking that
FAILURE IS PART OF THE PROCESS OF LEARNING.
We intrinsically know that to master a thing, you must first
fail at that thing—perhaps many times. Yet, we also know
that each failure provides us with a little more
information, information that will help us make a better
decision the next time we try that thing—whatever it
might be.

We are Resilient without naming it, which is both a
blessing and a curse. It's a blessing in our infancy and
early years, when we try and try and try, without

consciously calling on a skill (Resilience) that comes so naturally to us. But as we get older, as failure takes on new meaning—F A I L U R E!!!!!— we forget that we possess Resilience. Failure becomes something fraught with shame, and we stay in the place of not succeeding because trying again makes us vulnerable to other people's criticisms, scorn, and laughter.

How many times have you not tried something because you were afraid you'd be laughed at? Let's go out on a limb and say dozens, at least, especially during your teenage years. Did you think there was anything worse than being embarrassed in front of your peers as a teenager?

Think About It:

- Can you recall a time when you didn't try something because you were afraid of being laughed at or failing?

- Do you regret not trying?

- Would you try now if you could?

Here's a newsflash—no one has ever died of embarrassment. You may have felt like you were going to die, but surprise! You're still here. Of course, it doesn't feel good, but to not try something you genuinely want to do because you're afraid you'll look stupid, well, that's just stupid. Because you've already looked stupid at something. We all have. That ship sailed long ago.

In fact, if you counted all of the times you looked stupid, you might actually die of embarrassment. Kidding. What you'd actually discover is your inexhaustible well of Resilience, because you've failed hundreds, if not thousands of times already, and yet you get up every day and live your life.

Are you afraid of looking stupid?
You've already looked stupid; we all have.
It's time to let it go.

Mary Fran Bontempo

Welcome to Resilience. Now that you know you've got it, the key is to use it effectively, strategically, to move you in the direction you want to go. But first, it's helpful to remind yourself of those instances when you were Resilient without recognizing what it was at the time.

Think About It:

- When did you experience a challenge, one you may have thought was something you'd never get past or survive, and even if you did, life would never be quite the same, or as good, again?

- Was your crisis long ago, or more recent? How did you get through the challenge? Looking back, can you identify any skills that helped you cope and move through to the other side? (Listening, organizing, developing short-term solutions to cope in the moment.)

CHAPTER 3

Time to Grow!

Examining our train wrecks and sucker punches from a distance allows us to put down the emotional baggage they created and think: How the hell did I get through that? We can dissect what we did and how we did it when the emotional fires burn down into embers instead of a raging inferno.

Our instinct in crisis is usually to put our heads down and plow through—the quicker the better. As Winston Churchill said, "If you're going through hell, *keep going*." While that may be exactly what's called for in our most challenging moments, a retrospective look back at your train wreck can yield all sorts of information about just how amazing you were during an absolutely horrible experience. And if you're not convinced that you're amazing, YOU ARE. Anyone who wades through giant piles of caca and comes out standing, or even crawling, is amazing. Pat on the back, you win, light up the fireworks--amazing. Own it.

Allow yourself the grace of time to heal—super important—and take a look back to see what you learned, because you did learn something, probably lots of things, although you may not have been aware of learning at the time. Challenges lead to change, and one change relevant to being Brilliantly Resilient is experiencing "post-traumatic growth" after a sucker punch or train wreck.

Psychology Today tells us that post-traumatic growth is defined as "positive psychological change experienced as a result of adversity and other challenges in order to rise to a higher level of functioning."

We love "science-y" definitions; they make us feel smart-ish. Basically, this means transformation after trauma. In Brilliantly Resilient terms, you can not only recover or bounce back from challenging circumstances (Resilience), you can use what you've learned to grow, create, and steer your life into highly fulfilling paths that you might not have dreamed of before your crisis (Brilliance). Not to get all Pollyanna-ish, but it's the silver lining you CREATE after a trauma that makes the difference.

> *We have to CREATE our silver linings,*
> *not just look for them.*

> Dr. David Fajgenbaum—Chasing My Cure

Creating our silver linings is making lemonade out of lemons. It's ACTIVE—a key to being Brilliantly Resilient. We take what we get, and we MAKE something out of it. That's so much more empowering than sitting around and waiting to see what happens.

But sometimes, we need a little help to make something happen, and that's okay, too. During your train wreck, you may have learned a specific new skill, one related to the challenge at hand but with applications beyond the situation. The skill need not be measurable in the traditional sense (we're not talking about mastering algebra), as long as it serves a valid purpose. For example, one of the most important skills both of us learned when faced with our respective sucker punches and train wrecks was the simple skill of raising our hands and asking for help.

Most of us are raised to value independence as a core strength for a well-adjusted adult. We like to grab a problem and handle it, saying, "I did it!" as a badge of honor. Look at me, the lone wolf of crisis, handling things myself! Yet when immersed in the whirlpool of a previously unknown trauma, singular triumph becomes less likely, especially if the challenge lies outside of our experience (i.e. blindness and heroin addiction).

In that case, acknowledging your empty crisis toolbox is essential. It's time to admit your lack of knowledge, your fear, and your utter inability to handle things on your own. While that may not sound like a newly learned skill to some, admitting that you're ill-prepared and need help, especially when you pride yourself on your independence, is not only a new experience, it's humbling and valuable both for managing the current scenario and those down the road.

Other post-traumatic growth changes can reflect things like a shift in perspective. A change in how we look at things naturally changes the way we respond. If, after trauma, someone experiences a greater appreciation of life, relationships, and previously under-appreciated blessings, that feeling will influence future decisions and behaviors, opening the door to new opportunities, and quite possibly leading to Brilliance. When you make it through something crazy hard and you're standing at the end of that road, appreciating newfound strength and determination can offer even more opportunities for living a Brilliantly Resilient life.

And let's not forget gratitude. Feelings of gratitude after managing a crisis are profound and can affect just about everything moving forward. Gratitude is one of the sharpest tools in our Brilliantly Resilient toolbox because after coming out blessed from our respective poopy shows, we're grateful to our Higher Power every single day.

Speaking of a Higher Power, we're card- carrying, shout-it-out-loud believers. The particulars don't matter to either of us; it's an awareness that when things were truly awful, someone or something carried us through. (Although in Kristin's case, it was more a drag while she kicked and screamed the entire time. A slightly different approach.)

Every bit of post-traumatic growth can encourage a willingness to explore, try new things, and collaborate with others—all of which show Resilience and can point the way to our Brilliance. To sum it up, here's our Brilliantly Resilient friend, Chip Baker, who says it in no uncertain terms:

You've got to grow through the go-through.

Chip Baker—The Success Chronicles

Think About It:

- After a trauma or challenge, did you experience any post-traumatic growth?

- What changed? How has the change affected you since?

CHAPTER 4

Have You Learned Nothing?

Learning a new skill while in the thick of a challenge or crisis is not unheard of. But there's another possibility: Maybe you didn't learn anything. At least not anything totally new. When we're hit with a sucker punch, we react based on the fight or flight instinct. While we'd love to run—who wouldn't want to jet away from a crisis—we usually end up fighting.

Given that the fight response is instinctive, and the need to respond to a crisis is usually immediate, there's not much time for learning something entirely new, or mastering a new skill to fix the current crisis.

The good news is you don't have to. This is where your stockpile of previously learned "stuff" comes into play. You already have a warehouse full of skills and talents that you bring to life every day. But like the way we think of Resilience, you aren't aware of these strategies because we rarely name them.

These are the things we're good at naturally, or perhaps things we've learned to be good at through prior experience, that move to the back of our brains in most everyday situations. While we can't speak for other cultures, we Americans tend to place a much higher value on things that are hard for us, believing that the more blood, sweat, and tears you have to expend on something, the more worthwhile it is. Consequently, we often brush off our natural skills and talents, believing that they have little value since we don't have to work at them.

Again, that's just stupid.

It's precisely those things that come naturally to us that best serve us during challenging times.

It's hard enough to deal with a train wreck without putting the added pressure on yourself to come up with an amazing new way to solve the problem. Odds are, you already have at least some skills and talents that will help you get a jump on the issue, initiating at least one action step that will move you towards a solution, or at least a mindset where you can think and begin to determine what's next.

These are called transferable skills, and the problem with defining them is that they don't come with a degree attached. It's not like saying, I'm an accountant, or a nurse, lawyer, or teacher. Yet each of those positions allows you to develop skills that are themselves transferrable, even though you may not be using them strictly in the context in which you developed them.

Think About It:

- Have you experienced Post-Traumatic Growth? (If you're thinking about being Brilliantly Resilient, the answer is likely, YES!)

- Did your growth manifest as a new skill, a new perspective, or a transferable skill?

If you're wondering, yes, we've experienced Post-Traumatic Growth, we've learned new skills, we've transferred others, and all of it happened during as well as after our respective sucker punches and train wrecks. It was a long and winding road, but one we need to travel, both apart and together, so here goes....

In Kristin's words:

Twenty years ago, I was living the dream. Married, beautiful McMansion home, expensive SUV, very comfortable bank account, and a beautiful first-born baby boy. (I often say that if I knew the old me now, I probably wouldn't like her very much!) Now, I am a divorced mom of three. Two of my children are blind. My bank accounts are depleted. However, I couldn't feel more blessed and I am the happiest I have ever been in my forty-nine years.

I am a planner. Like, shower and blow out my hair to take a special trip to Staples to flip through the planners for the upcoming year for HOURS, kind of planner. I love to create plans, goals, lists. Oh, and lists of my plans! Whether it's a five-year plan for a business idea or a five-item list for Costco, I friggin' love lists. But what I love the most about the list: Checking. Things. Off. And twenty years ago, I was well on my way to checking off the Kristin lifetime dream list.

I planned for pretty much my whole life to be a teacher. I knew from the time I was 5 years old that teaching would be my career. And while I planned to teach, I *dreamed* of becoming a mom. When I was in my late twenties and was glowing with my first pregnancy, my dreams for my baby grew as big as my belly grew. I envisioned a little boy with a big bright smile. A little girl with long black hair. Regardless of gender, I knew I'd give birth to the greatest athlete e-v-e-r. (Did I mention that I was a gifted athlete in school?) I daydreamed about football fields and soccer games, game-winning touchdowns, and grand slam home runs. I envisioned Prom, Valedictorian, Suma Cum Laude graduations.

On January 29, 2000, Michael arrived in the world. My life was perfect. Then, when Michael was five months old, in a tiny little hospital room in Philadelphia, a doctor told me, "Your son is blind." He told me there would be no baseball. No driving. My dreams and my body crashed to the floor.

I knew no one who was blind. NO ONE. I had zero frame of reference and no idea how to begin to help Michael live a happy, let alone successful, life. Where would I even start? I thought of myself—how would I function without my eyes? It simply wasn't possible that this was happening to me and my beautiful boy.

I fought and raged against blindness for three years, and through my second pregnancy. I'd learned that there was a twenty-five percent chance that each pregnancy could result in a baby being born with the same genetic defect Michael was afflicted by. But surely, God wouldn't do this to me or a new baby again.

Until He did. Mitchell was born three years after Michael, and Mitchell, too, was blind.

But just before Mitchell's birth, God sent me a gift through little Michael. You see, Michael wasn't bothered by blindness; I was. I had been praying for a miracle—and I intended that miracle to be sight. But we have our plans and God has His. The miracle I was blessed with was I finally realized that my son wasn't bothered by blindness. It was my perception of blindness that was holding him back. God did not cure Michael's vision, He cured mine.

That was the moment when I knew that I would find the tools necessary for my sons to succeed. They would be happy, productive, successful people. And I would help them get there.

In Mary Fran's words:

As a child, I grew up in Northeast Philadelphia, attending Catholic school from grade school right on through college. We were raised with a strong work ethic by a strong disciplinarian—my dad was large, loud, and more than a little scary. My mom, a tiny Italian lady, a full foot shorter than my brusque, German father, kept him, and us, in line.

In our middle-class neighborhood, we believed that if you worked hard and did the right thing, everything would be okay. Which I believed. Until it wasn't.

My son's addiction and alcoholism weren't the only train wrecks I had to manage in my adulthood, though they were by far the worst. There was also a fire that burned down our family business, a flood inside our house that destroyed all but one room, anxiety and depression that one time sent me to the hospital thinking I was having a stroke, and my father's sudden death from a brain aneurysm. And those are just the highlights.

But all of it paled in comparison to Mother's Day of 2010, when I learned that my son was a heroin addict.

We were visiting my mother—my family and one of my brothers and his kids—when I heard a commotion coming from the family room. I rushed in to see my son sitting on the couch shaking uncontrollably. We called the paramedics, who repeatedly asked him what he had taken, a question I didn't understand at the time. It wasn't until they got David in the ambulance that he confessed he'd taken a painkiller he stole in an attempt to get the high he usually got from heroin. Once we got to the hospital, doctors told us that if they couldn't reverse the effects of the medicine he'd ingested, he would need a liver transplant—if he lived.

Have you ever had one of those moments when someone is speaking to you, saying words that you know are in your native language, and you understand them as individual words, but they make no sense as complete sentences? I remember hearing the doctor tell me my son was a heroin addict and that he might need a liver transplant, but I didn't understand him. I simply couldn't process what he was saying. After he repeated the information, I remember feeling as though I were watching myself in some wakeful nightmare—there, but not. That feeling people talk about where everything slows to a crawl is real. When someone tells you that your child's life is on the line, everything changes in an instant.

Don't get me wrong. I didn't have a perfect kid one day and the next had a heroin addict. I knew there were problems, but I had no idea how serious they were. When dealing with a crisis, especially addiction, I often say a parent's two closest companions are denial and distraction, and I'd let both control my thinking for far too long. It wasn't until the overdose that I had to look truth square in the face.

That day marked the end of everything I thought I knew about myself—who I was, where I'd been, where I was going. I've always loved the movie *The Wizard of Oz,* and this was like my own personal tornado—without Emerald City at the end. Addiction tore through everything and would continue to do so for a very long time.

David survived the overdose, without needing a liver transplant, thank God. But that was just the beginning of a journey down a dark and winding road with no clear direction towards the finish line, if there was a finish line that didn't end with my child losing his life.

Every parent of an addict would throw themselves under a bus to save their kid, if only that would work. But it doesn't, so we're left to try and cobble together answers and solutions that won't matter at all until the addict is ready to commit to treatment. But as parents, we have to try. We couldn't live with ourselves if we didn't.

With time of the essence, I unconsciously began diving into my natural skill set, using talents that came easily to me to keep my own nose above water and to hold up my son long enough to get him help.

Now for our Brilliantly Resilient Collaboration:

This is where, as we got to know each other better, our stories began to converge. Not the details, of course; those were wildly different. But the need to find answers in crises to save our children gave us a common foundation that transcended the details. As we talked about how we had helped our kids, we realized that we both called forth our natural skill sets without consciously being aware of doing so. Those skills and talents became the basis for finding our way through challenges and creating life beyond. Eventually, we realized the role of Resilience and Brilliance in our somewhat bumbling efforts, and Brilliantly Resilient was born.

CHAPTER 5

Is Anybody Out There?

Let us re-emphasize something that's become our go-to over the years: We learned to put up our hands and ask for help. We Americans, in addition to believing that anything worthwhile has to be hard, also believe fiercely in independence. It's a badge of honor for us to be able to say, "Lookee here—I did it myself and nobody helped me!" Well, good for you, but in our experience, if you had asked for help and ACCEPTED IT, whatever you just did would likely have been exponentially, or at least somewhat, better.

We hold a "certification" of which we are most proud. We are Doctors of Nothing. Since we readily admit that we don't know a lot, it allows us to form amazing collaborations and wonderful partnerships with super cool, smart people. Even in our areas of Brilliance, we know that there's always more to learn, which has been one of the great joys of Brilliantly Resilient. We never actually arrive; there's always new and fascinating stuff to add to the treasure trove of Brilliance.

By acknowledging our "ignorance," we also kept our

brains and our hearts prepped to receive information, support, and peace. When you're thrust into a crisis, peace is the last thing you feel. Yet, to make productive decisions, you have to arrive at, if not a place of calm, at least not a place of AAAAAAAHHHHHHHH! IT'S THE END OF THE WORLD!!!!! No one ever accomplishes anything sustainable when you act as if your hair's on fire.

The simple awareness that there are others out there who have more experience and knowledge than you, and can offer you a bucket of water to manage the blaze, is a gateway to tapping into your own Resilience and opening the door to sharing your Brilliance. When we acknowledge that people before us have dealt with some version of our train wreck and survived, we signal to our brains that all is not lost, and there is a path through.

As our Brilliantly Resilient friend and founder of HIP Chicks, Beth Allen, notes,

> *Doing it yourself doesn't mean doing it alone.*
>
> Beth Allen—HIP Chicks

Yup.

Let's take a quick detour here. Notice that we said a path "through," not forward. We don't always get to go forward, even though running headlong past our troubles is what everyone wants. But…

*Life is a series of dance moves. You move forward, you
move back, and sometimes you just stay in place,
swaying from side to side.*

Mary Fran Bontempo

Sometimes, our Resilience must translate into staying power, because occasionally, time is the answer. Resilience may mean you do your best to stand upright, occasionally stumbling, moving with the wind of circumstances, and letting your problem unknot itself over time.

But even time can be helped along by others.

Enter the tribe.

When we think of our tribe—a.k.a. our family and friends, our community, our co-workers—we usually think of those we know. In other words, our first-level contacts. First-level contacts are the people who are closest to us, the ones who know us best, due to time or circumstance. And yes, those folks are essential to our lives. They are the ones we know will be there—always, no matter what we need. So of course they're the only ones we would rely on in a crisis, right?

Well, no. While our nearest and dearest can support us in ways no one else can, there is a downside to all of that closeness. We see those we love through the lens of our experiences with them, the unique way we know them. That experience doesn't always allow for a complete picture, especially if we've known someone for a long time.

Have you ever gone home for a holiday with siblings and found yourself regressing into roles you played long ago, assuming that the brother or sister you grew up with is the same exact person you fought with over which television show to watch? (Yes, we're that old.) We don't allow for the growth that's happened since our childhoods. Sometimes, that happens with those to whom we are closest, which means when we only turn to those we know best for help, they, and we, may be missing something—or a lot of somethings, which doesn't help our cause.

That's why it's essential, when experiencing a crisis in which you have a depleted toolbox, to open your ranks instead of closing them around you for protection.

Put up your hand. Whether you ask a friend if they know someone who can help with xzy, or you do some internet digging to find an organization or service with experience dealing with your train wreck, or you research your LinkedIn connections, someone out there who never crossed your mind may hold the key to that first step forward.

Kristin learned the power of the "raise hand, help please" strategy a few years into her journey with raising blind kiddos. She found one mom, Kay Leahy, that had raised a blind child to be successful and witty, charming and thriving, and asked her how she could guide her boys in the same way. Kristin literally raised her hand during a presentation Kay was giving and asked her how she could stop crying every day and move toward thriving. That first hand raise led to Kristin doing it again and again, finding and asking blind role models for guidance with her boys.

The results of that strategy have been extraordinary.

Yes, we are Doctors of Nothing. But we know doctors. And teachers, and entrepreneurs, and Emmy winning journalists, and corporate CEOs, and artists, and lawyers, and so many, many people who have helped us over the years to become even more Brilliantly Resilient, because we asked them for help.

Put up your hand. Someone out there will see you.

CHAPTER 6

Still Figuring It Out

Time and repetition. When we talk about being Brilliantly Resilient, it's essential to know that we're talking about a process—one that we both repeat over and over, every single day, because we're still working on it, and will be—forever. We "get it," but we haven't "gotten it." We understand, but we haven't arrived at a permanent place of Brilliance and Resilience, because it doesn't exist.

If you've ever practiced yoga, you'll know that even the most proficient yogis refer to yoga as a practice. They know without a doubt that every day is different, every experience "doing yoga" is different, and every session is an opportunity to learn something new.

So it is with being Brilliantly Resilient. We all have the capacity to be Brilliantly Resilient but let's be serious, some days we're more Brilliantly Resilient than others. In fact, Kristin has been known to cry in her car in the parking lot at Costco, and Mary Fran has night terrors and occasionally wakes up screaming in the middle of the night. Too much information? Sorry, but being Brilliantly

Resilient sometimes means being brutally honest. We don't have everything figured out, we don't skip through every day encased in circles of golden light, and our kids still think we're crazy. We cry, we have tantrums, we shake our fists at God. (And then we apologize because do we need any more crap dumped on our heads?)

But we don't live there. That is the first and perhaps most important decision you can make when claiming the Brilliantly Resilient title as your own. Everyone, and we mean EVERYONE, has stuff. Sticky, yucky, miserable stuff.

Sometimes life just sucks. The question is, are you just visiting, or are you going to live there?

Mary Fran Bontempo

One of the most important steps in being Brilliantly Resilient is to make the conscious decision that you aren't unpacking your bags, setting up camp, and living in your yuck. So much of being Brilliantly Resilient starts in the six inches between your ears. We don't want to veer into Woo-woo territory (Mary Fran hates the Woo-woo territory), but unless you set intentions and decide what you want and don't want, you'll stay stuck in the yuck.

Yes, it's happening, yes, you have to deal with it, but it doesn't have to become your entire story. It is part of your story, and what you incorporate into your life is entirely up to you. You get to choose whether you incorporate the lessons and then move on to create your Brilliance, or whether you internalize the misery and play the victim. Here's a hint: pick the first option. The sucker punch is only the end if you decide it is. Listen to Nicole Simonin, founder of Shape It Up Fitness:

> *We get to choose whether we get knocked out,*
> *whether we get stunned,*
> *or whether we get up again.*

Nicole Simonin—Shape It Up Fitness

Oh, we love that!!! When Nicole first voiced the idea on our show, Brilliantly Resilient LIVE, we almost jumped out of our seats. Yes, yes, YES!!!! We CHOOSE. We still get hit, but we get to choose how we respond. How Brilliantly Resilient is that?

Now, let's not sugar-coat things. The punch is still gonna suck. You find yourself suddenly single, the bank is calling, the diagnosis is not good. Whatever the details, you are going to be stunned. And that's okay. Under no circumstances do we want anyone to think you aren't entitled to feel beat up or bludgeoned by your challenges. In fact, you must acknowledge and honor your feelings; it's the only way to work through the emotional baggage that accompanies every sucker punch and train wreck. We're champs at acknowledging our feelings. We're so good at it that we've turned ranting, raving, and fist-shaking into an art form.

So have at it. Be stunned, be furious, be sad. Cry, rage, and swear (one of us is particularly good at the swearing part, and it's not who you might think...). Go all-in on your personal pity party. And then...

STOP.

Do not dig a hole, fill it with a nice, squishy bean bag chair, and plop your butt in it. You will never get out.

Think About It:

- When you experienced a sucker punch or train wreck, did you whine, cry and feel sorry for yourself? (It's okay to answer, "YES!")

- How long did your pity party last? What did you do to move forward?

Feeling sorry for ourselves is a comfortable place to be, believe it or not. When we're experiencing our train wrecks, not only do we feel bad for ourselves, so do other people. And we get a pass. We're forgiven for our lousy moods and our lack of contribution to the betterment of the world. People figuratively stoke our heads and think, Oh poor baby. Look at what s/he is going through. No one makes demands on us because they figure we've got as much as we can possibly handle.

Ahhhhh. What a lovely spot. But notice how comfy

your butt is there? YOU'VE GOT TO GET OUT!!! Get out now, before misery becomes your permanent state of mind. Because after a while, those folks who felt sorry for you are going to decide that they want no parts of your victim mentality and your poor me attitude. We all know that person who acts like the world is out to get them. Well, guess what? It's out to get all of us. But the likelihood of it catching you decreases exponentially if you don't sit there waiting for bad stuff to happen.

Now move. Give yourself a limited time to whine and then stop it. Mary Fran is The 15 Minute Master. You've got fifteen minutes to hold a drive—through pity party. Then, get on with it. Be stunned. We'd worry about you if you weren't. But don't get knocked out. Get up. Again, and again, AND AGAIN.

CHAPTER 7

Make the Choice

Okay, it's decision time again. To be Brilliantly Resilient, you must repeatedly remind yourself that you have a choice. Not a choice about your circumstances, but a choice about how those circumstances will be incorporated into the rest of your life. This is a big one, so pay attention here. You must decide:

> *Do you want to come through*
> *"Broken or Brilliant?"*

> Kristin Smedley

It's entirely your decision. Again, you will likely come through banged up, bruised, and bent. But that's not broken. Broken is destroyed, and you never have to let your circumstances destroy you, even when it seems they will.

You will still be able to pick up the pieces, create something new—remember, nothing stays the same—and Rise. But you must decide to come through Brilliant, not

Broken.

If you go about your challenges intentionally seeing them as opportunities for growth instead of setups to fail, the Reset and Rise are easier. You're well on the way to tapping into your Brilliance. But first, it's time to give up—sort of.

There is something to be said for giving up. Well, not exactly giving up. There's one little word missing from that sentiment. You aren't "Giving up," you're "Giving IT up."

Do you see the difference? Giving up means throwing in the towel: I'm outta here; I ain't doing this anymore. Giving IT up means turning your train wreck over to your Higher Power, or the universe, or time, or whatever you believe in. It means doing everything possible to improve the situation, but acknowledging that when it's out of your control, it's time to "Let it go!" in the immortal words of Elsa from Frozen. It's time to surrender.

Surrender gets a bad rap. It doesn't necessarily mean defeat. Surrender provides space for breathing room, acceptance, and can even open the door to opportunities where no door existed before. Surrender allows us to replenish our energy to come back to the situation with hopeful eyes and new ideas. Or, it allows us to move on. Both options are valid responses to challenges. We simply have to be aware of the value and relevance of each.

When we give IT up, allow the powers that be, or the universal energy, or whatever, to have its say, we're offered one of the keys to Brilliance. That doesn't mean that when you throw up your hands and say, "Okay, God; tag, you're it!" and surrender to the Almighty that you'll be gifted with one of those Aha moments that everyone talks about and suddenly you'll have everything figured out. Rather, when we allow things to unfold and evolve, after putting in our best efforts and not being married to an outcome, something, or nothing, will happen. Once it does, or doesn't, once we've let go of trying to force everything to turn out the way WE WANT IT TO, then we can see what worked, what didn't, and how our efforts fit into the picture.

It also means that when you've done all you can, you can drop the rock and see what else could be out there that might catch your eye or engage your mind. It's a big world, and when you finally stop running into the brick wall, your vision may clear just enough to see something else, something incredibly cool, that makes you realize the initial crisis wasn't the end of the world to begin with.

Have the fluidity to follow where the universe is guiding you.

Violette de Ayala—Founder, FEM City

One of Mary Fran's best friends, Chris Cherwien, was a pillar of strength during Mary Fran's struggles with her son David's addiction. Chris continually told M.F., "This, too, shall pass." While that advice didn't "solve" anything, it did allow Mary Fran to give herself a break from the constant worry and heartache of her experience.

That bit of breathing room, the place where we allow ourselves to rest in knowing that we've done what we could and it's out of our hands, can be the very moment when we open the door to discovering our Brilliance and looking towards the future the universe sees for us, even if we can't see it ourselves.

Do what you can, then give it up.

CHAPTER 8

Aha, Schmaha!

Since we've brought up the Aha moment, let's be clear: not everyone has one. In fact, even if we do, that doesn't mean it's going to be a life-changing epiphany.

When big stuff happens, we tend to think it's going to take a big solution to fix it. Yet, more often than not, there is no big fix. Rather, it's the series of small, constructive changes that ultimately bring about a resolution. While crisis can overtake us with a frightening leap that changes our lives, the path forward is usually much more measured, often taking shape one next step at a time.

One of our guests on Brilliantly Resilient LIVE was Mary Fran's son David, who struggled with substance abuse issues for many years. During the interview, Kristin asked David if he could identify the moment when everything turned around for him. Did he have an Aha moment? "No," he responded. "I just got to a point where I felt I was done and knew I had to start to do things differently."

I didn't have an epiphany.
I just knew I had to start doing things differently.

David Bontempo—Proudly in Recovery

Did you just breathe a sigh of relief? We live in a culture where we believe events must be big to have value. We are Americans, after all. Bigger is always best, except when it isn't. You don't need big to know it's time for change. What you need is to listen to that small voice inside (you know, the one that lives in the pit of your stomach), that says, "Hey! Hey you! In case you haven't realized it, this is not where we need to be. It's time to get out of here."

Let's say it again: YOU DON'T NEED AN EPIPHANY. Nor do you need a major crisis like blindness or addiction to know you're not where you need to be. Many of us live what we consider to be ordinary lives. We're grateful that we have no major trauma, but we aren't content. We feel like something's missing, but then we feel guilty for not appreciating the fact that we haven't experienced a major train wreck, so we push the discontent aside, allowing it to simmer every day just beneath the surface.

That's exhausting. It can be just as exhausting as battling a major crisis. It can also lead to underlying depression and anxiety, so do not ignore it. If you're feeling your life isn't what it could be, then DO SOMETHING about it.

Think About It

- Have you ever had an Aha moment? What about?

- Have you never had an Aha moment? Do you feel you've missed something?

Brilliance can start small; it's a choice, just like Resilience. Brilliance begins by listening to that voice, that tug that's pulling you in a direction and won't let you go, even when you want it to. Brilliance starts by paying attention—to what you're good at, to what comes easily to you, to what others ask for your help with.

Paying attention isn't easy, especially in a world where our attention is splintered by ever-present demands of technology pinging, binging, and shrieking to be noticed, along with our work demands, family demands, and life demands.

Yet, that's precisely why we MUST pay attention— to ourselves. One of the reasons so many people never find their Brilliance is that it requires self-reflection and introspection, which requires quiet—something in rare supply. We must shut down the noise, whether it's actual noise or the figurative sort, manifesting in our heads as the endless list of things we "have to do" to get through our day.

Unfortunately, that endless list too often becomes an excuse. How often have you uttered the words, "I don't have time"? Sorry, but we call B.S. Even five minutes a day spent thinking about YOU— what makes you amazing (and yes, there is much) will help lead you on the path towards your Brilliance. We need to take the time to uncover the best parts of ourselves, our gifts, those things we're supposed to share with the world. It's your greatest responsibility, and it's why you're here.

Align your personal gifts with your style and with your desire to bring your Brilliance.

Kathy Nimmer
—Award-Winning Teacher,
Huffington Post Writer

You, thinking about you, paying attention to what you're feeling, good, bad or in-between, will be the catalyst for making changes—big or small. Remember: The small ones can be just as significant as the big ones, especially if you're committed and consistent. Bigger isn't always better. Your "Aha!" may be small, until it starts to change everything.

CHAPTER 9

It Ain't Rocket Science

Here's the good news: your Brilliance IS NOT HARD, at least not for you. That doesn't mean the world will welcome it immediately and you'll make a zillion dollars and live happily ever after once you acknowledge it and allow it to bloom. It does mean that you'll feel a sense of peace, fulfillment, and joy unlike anything you've experienced before, EVEN WHEN YOU SCREW UP. Because you will screw up, even though it's your Brilliance.

Sound contradictory? Well, yes and no. (We love when it sounds like we aren't making sense. Wait for it...)

Cultivating your Brilliance is a journey, a process, one that must be explored. You'll make mistakes, but remember, mistakes are and have always been part of the process of learning. Mistakes teach us what works, what doesn't, and allow us to move ahead. Without mistakes, nothing happens.

Mary Fran tells the story of a time at the beach when

she was building a sandcastle with her then five-year-old granddaughter, Emma. It was a drip castle—the kind where you take a handful of wet sand and slowly drip it onto the castle. Drip castles are a slow process, and Emma was getting impatient. So, she decided to get a shovel of wet sand and dump it onto the delicate drip castle, effectively crushing it.

Instead of crying, throwing a tantrum, and giving up on the entire enterprise, Emma looked at her efforts, said, "Well, that didn't work," and went on to try another method to build her castle.

Out of the mouths of babes. Talk about a revelation. In four little words, a child summed up what our attitude should be about making mistakes. "Well, that didn't work," so TRY SOMETHING ELSE. Brilliance is eventually uncovered after trying, saying, "Well, that didn't work," and trying something different. Every single thing humanity has ever discovered or created has been a result of that process.

No one, and we mean NO ONE, is Brilliant without failure. We intrinsically know this as kids. Kids never, ever fail at something and are ashamed of that failure. They know that success is a process. It's not until we adults teach them that mistakes are wrong that kids feel shame in failing and then stop trying.

Good God stop already. Stop thinking that you aren't made of the stuff of Brilliance. We all are. When we started our Brilliantly Resilient LIVE World Takeover Tour (Yes, that's what we called it. Go big or go home.) it began with a wildly successful live kickoff event. We planned to

48

take the program on the road, teaching live audiences how to uncover their own Brilliance and Resilience.

We all know how that went. Pandemic, no tour, buh-bye plan, nothing. We went from congratulating ourselves on our success to sitting in our respective offices, staring at our computers, and wondering how the heck we were going to salvage what we knew needed to get out to the world. Having each failed spectacularly more times than either of us could count, we simply decided to put on a live show via a streaming platform. No big plan, just hey, let's try this and see what happens.

So, we did. We figured it out along the way. Some stuff worked, some didn't, and we tweaked it as we went along, sharing our efforts in real-time with our audience intentionally, to prove that Brilliance and Resilience all start with trying something, anything, and moving forward from there.

Try something, see where it lands, and go from there.

Kristin Smedley &
Mary Fran Bontempo

You'll find bits of Brilliance along the way, which is part of the joy of the whole process. When something works, there's little that is more fun than whooping it up and crowing, "Oh my god, can you believe how cool that was?!!!" Even the screw-ups have provided us with more than a few giggles. When you allow yourself to settle into the process, both the successes and the failures are gifts to expand your knowledge and help you hone your Brilliance. Take it from Melinda Emerson, aka SmallBizLady:

Success leaves clues everywhere, but so does failure.

Melinda Emerson—SmallBizLady

If you're still not sure where to start to uncover your Brilliance, look around you. Start with who you are, who you thought you were going to be, and what you learned to get there.

Both of us have degrees as educators. We're teachers by education, and that's what we both figured we would do professionally. Yeah. Apparently, the universe had other plans, because although we both did spend time in front of the classroom, neither of us had the traditional teaching career we'd envisioned. Note the use of the word, "traditional."

As life hit us with its train wrecks and sucker punches, we found ourselves managing and coping by relying on skills we had honed for other purposes. We were good at school; learning was kind of our jam. So when hit with our cosmic smackdowns, we both (and remember, this was long before we'd met) set out to learn everything we could about blindness (Kristin's sucker punch), and addiction (Mary Fran's train wreck).

We were smart enough to know what we didn't know, which was pretty much everything, about either issue, and we were great at asking questions. So, we found people who did know and proceeded to create teams of experts who could guide us along the way. And then, we LISTENED TO THEM, continuing to ask questions, learn, and implement our action steps based on new knowledge and the help of the communities we'd built for ourselves and our children.

Sounds like an amazing plan, doesn't it? We would claim full credit, if only we'd had a clue that it's what we were doing at the time. Truthfully, we were both in survival mode, too stunned to figure out much of anything, let alone a carefully crafted plan. And that's the beauty of it.

Both of us, without knowing what we were doing, relied on our natural skill sets as students and teachers to learn all we could about our crises, and then implemented a plan to help both our kids and us. But make no mistake, there was no conscious thought dictating that we would do step one, then step two, and so on. Our actions were based on the skills and talents that came easily to us— learning, studying, organizing, building a team, and working with that team towards a positive outcome.

Sound anything like what a teacher does? It was. And utilizing those natural skills, almost without thinking, became the best way for us to ultimately make the difference between helping our kids and just crawling into bed and pulling the covers over our heads.

Think About It:

- What are you naturally good at?

- What do others regularly ask for your help with?

- Do people ask to "pick your brain?" (We hate that saying, but do they?) What about?

Want to know what your Brilliance is? Answer the questions above. Really. Stop reading ahead if you always skip over questions in books because you think you'll do it later. We know you never do, because neither do we. Your Brilliance is there. It's in you. It's always been. In fact, it's been by your side and so much a part of you that you may have been ignoring it or taking it for granted.

STOP IT, ALREADY!

Your Brilliance deserves to be recognized. Shouted from the rooftops, Woohoo, look at me, recognized. Recognizing your Brilliance is the first step in respecting your Brilliance, and your Brilliance deserves respect.

Both of us use faith as a tool in our Brilliantly Resilient journeys. We hold onto our faith with white-knuckled grips, because without faith, we'd both be giant puddles of goo right about now. Just as the gift of faith must be respected, so must the gift of your Brilliance, because that's your unique tool—the one God gave specifically to you to share with the world. That's a gift that demands respect.

God will honor that gift, too. It was given to you for a reason. God actually wants you to succeed, because if you don't, you screw up the Divine Plan. But be prepared to walk a crooked path. Rarely is the thing you put in motion going to succeed the first time and exactly the way you've envisioned.

We've become accustomed to starting things, only to have them take a wild detour, only to have them work out even better than we could have imagined in the end, because after ranting a bit, we get a grip on ourselves, look to the heavens and say, "Okay, FINE, God! If this is the way you want it, FINE. But you'd better be there to help us figure this out!" (We said we're ranting experts.) And surprise, or not, God comes through. Every. Single. Time. Even if it's in a way we never expected.

Cease striving and know that I am God.

Psalm 46:10

Your Brilliance is in you. And you're amazing at it.

CHAPTER 10

The Next Steps

This is where it all begins. Knowing that we are all Brilliantly Resilient. Every single one of us. Resilience is inside of us; we rely on it regularly as children even though we don't name it. But it's there. And it will be there to serve you whenever you need it, but you have to remember to call it out. Know it, believe it, and it will serve you.

The same goes for your Brilliance. It's your unique gift or talent, and it's unique because of what YOU bring to it. Yes, there will always be others who do what you do, but NO ONE will do it exactly as you do. It's all about you, baby.

Brilliance and Resilience—there for the taking. But first, have a look at what our buddy, Tyler J. McCall asks:

Is the past that you had what you want for your future?

Tyler J. McCall —Founder,
Online Business Association

As we've said before, and will continue to say until we remember it, (yes, we need to remind ourselves of how to be Brilliantly Resilient—same as you), everything is precipitated by a CHOICE. You must choose to be Brilliantly Resilient. Once you do, you can begin to learn and work the steps and strategies that will help you create a life that's Brilliant, not broken. You MUST believe it's possible. Tiffany Smiley, who nursed her husband Scott after a suicide car bomb in Iraq took his eyesight and has gone on to build an inspirational organization of hope with Scott, puts it this way:

> *I believed in my vision of the future*
> *more than in anyone else's doubt.*

> Tiffany Smiley —Speaker,
> Founder, More Than Me

It took both of us a long time to figure this stuff out. When we finally met each other and realized that we'd managed our respective sucker punches and train wrecks in ways that were so similar that there was actually a kind of process involved, it was revelatory. (We kind of wish we'd recorded the moment when it finally hit us that we were onto something. It was a combination of the Dumb and Dumber guys figuring something out and the Minions saying, "WWHHHAAAAATTTTT???!!")

Now that we know we're Brilliantly Resilient, we know that you can be too, and there is a process that we can teach you, that we want to share. And share, and share, and share, because we don't want anyone (even people we don't like so much) to feel as crappy as we did for as long as we did.

In this series, you'll learn that becoming Brilliantly Resilient is a three-step process, which is simple, although not necessarily easy. (Not the same thing, remember?) To be Brilliantly Resilient, you'll have to:

RESET, RISE,
and REVEAL your BRILLIANCE

Easy, right? Not so fast. As with everything that sounds too good to be true, it is. You don't just master a three-piece mantra and suddenly become Brilliantly Resilient. Each phase contains several pieces—simple pieces, but not easy—that must be understood and worked through, one at a time, before you get to steer your own Brilliantly Resilient ship.

Remember also that this isn't always about experiencing a massive sucker punch. We want to show you how to navigate not only through a crisis, but everyday challenges as well, because sometimes the cumulation of everyday beatdowns can be just as devastating as a train wreck. Your challenges are uniquely yours, and big or small, they can be managed to help you uncover your Brilliantly Resilient self. (However, make no mistake, if you're making a mountain out of a molehill, we will kick you in the butt and tell you to knock it off. Well, Mary Fran will. Kristin will hand you the ice pack for your bruised ego.)

When you join us on this journey, you'll not only learn how to master the steps to become Brilliantly Resilient, you'll hear more from our amazing Brilliantly Resilient LIVE show guests— folks who are Brilliantly Resilient in their own right and who have created Brilliantly Resilient lives following the same steps we did, although none of us knew each other at the time.

Every single person we've met has gone through their version of the process we've used to become Brilliantly Resilient, which proves to us that as we've detailed the strategies followed in our journeys, they work. It's not only possible for you, but it's also doable, empowering, fascinating, and yes, fun. (We don't do anything unless it's fun.)

So, check out the next few pages for ways to keep in touch with us, learn more, and get the details on our Brilliantly Resilient contributors. Then, we want to help you get started on your Brilliantly Resilient journey, so we've added a few pages to get you thinking on some of the topics we've discussed and take some notes. Underline stuff inside, jot down your thoughts, questions (email us at howdy@brilliantlyresilient.net) and whatever else moves you, and get going. It's time for you to be Brilliantly Resilient!

A final message from Mary Fran & Kristin
(scan the QR code for the video message!)

So, get ready to RESET, RISE, and REVEAL your
BRILLIANCE! Here is some help to get you started:

- Read the BRILLIANTLY RESILIENT, RESET, RISE and REVEAL your BRILLIANCE series of books

- Join our Facebook Community

- https://www.facebook.com/groups/Brilliantly Resilient/

- Visit the Brilliantly Resilient website at www.brilliantlyresilient.net

- Subscribe to the Brilliantly Resilient newsletter at www.brilliantlyresilient.net

- Watch our Brilliantly Resilient LIVE show on Facebook
- Subscribe to the Brilliantly Resilient YouTube channel - https://tinyurl.com/brillent

Yep, there are a lot of opportunities to become Brilliantly Resilient. But remember, you don't just become Brilliantly Resilient and stay there. We work at it every single day.

We know our Brilliance. But we didn't always. And if you'd like to uncover your own Brilliance and Resilience, we can show you how. Join us, follow, learn, grow, RESET, RISE, and REVEAL, and let's be BRILLIANTLY RESILIENT together!

Learn more about Brilliantly Resilient by following us at:

Website:
http://www.brilliantlyresilient.net/

Facebook:
https://www.facebook.com/groups/BrilliantlyResilient

Instagram:
https://www.instagram.com/brilliantlyresilient/

Our Brilliantly Resilient
Superstar Contributors!

Beth Allen: Author—Flush the Fear,
Founder— HIP Chicks, https://diyhipchicks.com

Chip Baker: Founder—The Success Chronicles,
https://chip-baker-the-success-chronicles.square.site/

The Bible: Version, your choice!

David Bontempo, Jr.
dbtresourcesllc@gmail.com

Mary Fran Bontempo:
Speaker, Author, Virtual Presenter, Resilience Rock Star,
https://maryfranbontempo.com/

Violette de Ayala: Founder, FemCity,
https://www.violettedeayala.com/

John Lee Dumas
Founder/Host, Entrepreneurs On Fire,
https://www.eofire.com

Melinda Emerson SmallBizLady,
https://succeedasyourownboss.com/

Dr. David Fajgenbaum Author—Chasing My Cure,
https://chasingmycure.com/about/

Tyler J. McCall   Instagram Guru,
https://www.tylerjmccall.com/

Kathy Nimmer Teacher, Author,
https://www.amazon.com/Minutes-Eternity-Light- Kathy-Nimmer/dp/1598582542

Ming Shelby Courage Up Podcast,
https://www.mingshelby.com/

Nicole Simonin Founder—Shape It Up Fitness,
https://shapeitupfitness.com/

Kristin Smedley
Speaker, Author, Virtual Presenter, Resilience
Rock Star, http://kristinsmedley.com/

Tiffany Smiley:
Speaker, Founder—More Than Me,
https://tiffanysmiley.com/

To inquire about speaking engagements, workshops, or programs for your organization, contact us at: howdy@brilliantlyresilient.net.

We can't wait to be Brilliantly Resilient with you!

One More Thing

When we laid the groundwork for the program that would become Brilliantly Resilient at the end of 2019, we had no idea what was coming in 2020. All we knew was that our personal experiences with our respective train wrecks and sucker punches had equipped us with strategies, tools, sources, and a process to manage crisis.

We both felt "called" (again, big God believers, here), to do this work, to get Brilliantly Resilient out into the world. So we started to create, getting ready to launch in March of 2020 (which we somehow pulled off, again, nods to the Almighty), and after getting stopped in our tracks by a global pandemic, we realized that once again, God's plan was bigger than ours.

The creation of Brilliantly Resilient—the show, podcast and this book (the first of a series of four!) could not be timelier and more necessary. We are nowhere near out of the woods with COVID, and we honestly believe that there's a cosmic Brilliance that brought us together and allowed us to share Brilliantly Resilient with the world precisely at a time when the strategies we offer can help everyone as they helped us.

But COVID is simply the current crisis. There will be others, both large in scale and more personal, and you will face them. How you face them is the question. If we have anything to say about it, it will be as your Brilliantly Resilient self, with all the gifts you bring to your life and ours. We're honored you have joined us on this journey.

Notes

Use the following pages to jot down your thoughts, ideas, questions (and yes, feel free to reach out to us with your questions at howdy@brilliantlyresilient.net) and whatever else moves you. We've added a few starters at the top of each page, but this is about you, so have at it. Time to get Brilliantly Resilient!!!

In Chapter 1, we say that we all deserve "better." What does that mean to you? Any other Brilliantly Resilient thoughts?

_____

_____

_____

_____

_____

_____

_____

_____

Notes

What does Resilience mean to you and can you recall when you've used it in the past? Any other Brilliantly Resilient thoughts?

_____

_____

_____

_____

_____

_____

_____

_____

_____

Notes

Have you experienced post-traumatic growth? When? What did you learn? Any other Brilliantly Resilient thoughts?

_____

_____

_____

_____

_____

_____

_____

_____

_____

_____

Notes

Name as many "tribe members" as you can think of. Now think about where you might look to add new members to your tribe. Any other Brilliantly Resilient thoughts?

_____

_____

_____

_____

_____

_____

_____

_____

_____

_____

Notes

What's your Brilliance? This is no place to be shy or modest. Brag away!!! Any other Brilliantly Resilient thoughts?

_____

_____

_____

_____

_____

_____

_____

_____

_____

_____

Notes

The next two pages are all about you—write whatever floats your boat!

_____

_____

_____

_____

_____

_____

_____

_____

_____

_____

_____

_____

_____

_____

_____

_____

_____

Acknowledgements

In case we haven't made it clear by now, gratitude is a thing for us. We're grateful for almost everything—even our challenges, although we won't be so annoying as to call them blessings, because they sucked. But they were great teachers, and the reason we're both where we are today.

Yet, it's really the people in our lives, most importantly our families and those friends who have stood by us in all of the madness, who are the real reason we do what we do. If you'll bear with us, we each need a moment, so here goes:

From Mary Fran: Thank you first and foremost to my Higher Power, God, whatever you may choose to call Him/Her. Nothing is possible without your blessing.

Thanks to Dave, David and Kelly, Laura and Mike, Megan and Jimmy and the Bontempo grandkids: Emma, Luca, Jackson, Kaia, Nate, Grant and Noah, for their love, support, and for making me laugh. You are all the reason I get up in the morning. And Mom, I'm so lucky to have you.

To those friends who have always been so encouraging and cheered me on—Jennifer Gardella, Denice

Whiteley, Robyn Graham, Kathy Marcino, Beth Allen, Kathy Harold, Jenny Clarke, Sue Harrigan, Chris Cherwien, Chryssa Smith, Gina Rubel, Jamie Broderick, Sue Rocco, my grade school crew and many others, I am beyond grateful for your belief in me.

To our Brilliantly Resilient Community, you cannot imagine how much you've impacted my life.

And finally, to my Brilliantly Resilient partner, Kristin, you make me laugh until I'm snorting, you're one of the smartest people I know, you're true, genuine, authentic, and I'm blessed to have met you. Thank you for going on this journey with me.

From Kristin: Thank you to the inventor of soccer. I am so grateful that the sport I love gave me brilliant members of my tribe. Moe, Shannon, Sister Mary Erinhead, Ellis, and Susan Nicole: For more than a few decades you guys are the ones that have passed me the ball to take the big shots, picked me up after a huge loss, and will take someone out if they play dirty against me. I am a blessed girl to have you on my team for life.

Thanks to Staci for always talking me through my sucker punches and cheering insanely loud for my wins, Jen Gardella for bringing me and MFB together (what were you thinking??!!) and Agnes, the best buddy/therapist I could ever know, for always being at the ready for "therapy" and wake-up calls to stay aligned with my values.

Thank you to my Michael for showing me what resilience looks like every single day, to my Mitchell for making sure I laugh every single day, and to my Karissa for letting me be my incredibly weird self every single day, on every car ride, every sideline, everywhere – God help you!

Although I am still a little annoyed with Him for all the sucker punches, I do have to give God a shout out for blessing me with the two best people to learn how to be Brilliantly Resilient from: my parents. Mom and Dad, thanks for showing all of us how it's done, and for being my biggest cheerleaders along the way!

And to MFB: Well, it's official, God really does have a sick sense of humor. I mean, putting us – US… YOU and ME – together to change the world? I think His sense of humor is questionable, but His brilliance isn't. You make us a brilliant pair and there is absolutely no other person I would want to be on this World Domination Tour with than you (well, maybe LL Cool J…). My Reset & Rise have never been so fun as it is with you, and your kicking and pulling and shoving my brilliance out around every corner has changed my life!

Us again: Like we said, we're grateful beyond words for all of you, and frankly, everyone we've met on this journey, because all of our experiences have brought us here. Thank you and stay tuned, everyone; we're just getting started. Here's to being Brilliantly Resilient together!

About the Authors

Mary Fran Bontempo

Mary Fran Bontempo is an award-winning 2- time TEDx speaker, author, humorist, and media host who teaches audiences to uncover their Brilliance and Resilience 15 minutes at a time. A sought-after presenter, Mary Fran is author of *Brilliantly Resilient, The 15 Minute Master* and *The Woman's Book of Dirty Words*. She is co-founder of the Brilliantly Resilient platform and brand.

Mary Fran proves small changes can create life-altering transformations, allowing individuals to be positive and successful in a rapidly changing world. A Huffington Post, Thrive Global and Entrepreneur.com contributor, and columnist for numerous websites, Mary Fran created a life-affirming brand of wisdom and wit after meeting the challenge of her son's heroin addiction.

A frequent media guest and speaker audiences of all ages delight in her empowering and entertaining message.

Find her at http://www.maryfranbontempo.com/.

Kristin Smedley

With two of her three children born blind, Kristin Smedley was thrown into a mother's nightmare with her dreams for her sons' futures torn apart. Determined that her boys would become productive, vital individuals, Kristin dove headfirst into unnavigated waters to equip her sons with the skills and tools they needed to build successful, happy lives. Kristin partnered with Comcast to promote accessible equipment for the visually impaired, testified before the FDA on behalf of the first ever treatment for blindness, submitted the first legislation to Congress in US history in Braille advocating for better services for the blind, founded a non-profit for genetic disease research, delivered a TEDx talk to change perceptions of blindness, and published a best-selling book, *Thriving Blind*, showing both blind and sighted readers the possibilities that exist with imagination and determination. Kristin's boundless energy and generous spirit allow her to carry her message of empowerment and hope to audiences beyond the blind community through her motivational speaking and programs.

Find her at: http://www.kristinsmedley.com/